BUDDHISM
ORACLE

BUDDHISM
ORACLE

Wisdom for peace,
love and happiness

SOFAN CHAN

DEDICATION

These cards are dedicated to my life partner Rochman Reese and my children, Cassia, Jarrah and Ficus. You are my daily inspiration.

Heartfelt gratitude to my special friend Michelle Chant, whose love, trust and support has made these cards a reality.

Thank you to all the friends, staff and teachers at Nan Tien Institute and the Venerables at Nan Tien Temple for their advice, kindness and support on my Buddha path.

A Rockpool book
PO Box 252
Summer Hill NSW 2103
rockpoolpublishing.com

Follow us! f 📷 rockpoolpublishing
Tag your images with #rockpoolpublishing

First published in 2014 by Rockpool Publishing as *Buddhism Reading Cards*, ISBN 9781925017380

This edition published in 2023 by Rockpool Publishing
ISBN: 9781922785763
Copyright text and images © Sofan Chan 2023
Copyright design © Rockpool Publishing 2023

Edited by Megan English
Design by Sara Lindberg, Rockpool Publishing

Printed and bound in China
10 9 8 7 6 5 4 3 2 1

All rights reserved. No part of this publication may be reproduced, stored in a retrieval system, or transmitted in any form or by any means, electronic, mechanical, photocopying, recording or otherwise, without the prior written permission of the publisher.

DISCLAIMER: The Buddha's wisdom presented in this set of cards is but a quick and fun introduction as it would be impossible to encapsulate such a vast body of philosophy and doctrine developed over such a long period of time so briefly. The core principles of Buddha's teachings have therefore been simplified for easy and enjoyable reading, and you are encouraged to investigate the Buddhist texts in more detail if so interested.

CONTENTS

Introduction	1
About The Cards	2
How To Use The Cards	6

TRUTH CARDS

The Four Noble Truths	12
How To Work With The Truth Cards	13
1 Suffering	*14*
2 Attachment	*16*
3 Letting go	*18*
4 The path	*20*

PURITY CARDS

The Noble Eightfold Path	22
How To Work With The Purity Cards	23
5 Pure understanding	*24*
6 Pure thought	*26*
7 Pure speech	*28*
8 Pure action	*30*
9 Pure livelihood	*32*
10 Pure effort	*34*
11 Pure mindfulness	*36*
12 Pure concentration	*38*

CONTEMPLATION CARDS

The Eight Realisations — 40

How To Work With The Contemplation Cards — 41

- *13 Impermanence* — *42*
- *14 Awareness* — *44*
- *15 Desires* — *46*
- *16 Discipline* — *48*
- *17 Dharma* — *50*
- *18 Forgiveness* — *52*
- *19 Detachment* — *54*
- *20 Karma* — *56*

CULTIVATION CARDS

The Sixteen Virtues — 58

How To Work With The Cultivation Cards — 59

- *21 Self-acceptance* — *60*
- *22 Generosity* — *62*
- *23 Compassion* — *64*
- *24 Courage* — *66*
- *25 Patience* — *68*
- *26 Gratitude* — *70*
- *27 Happiness* — *72*
- *28 Truthfulness* — *74*
- *29 Loving-kindness* — *76*

30 Determination	*78*
31 Equanimity	*80*
32 Wisdom	*82*
33 Peace	*84*
34 Unconditional Love	*86*
35 Renunciation	*88*
36 Energy	*90*

ABOUT ...

Buddha	92
Your Buddha Nature	93
Mindfulness	95
Meditation	97
The Author And Artist: Sofan Chan	99
Sources And Resources	101

INTRODUCTION

'By your own efforts, waken yourself, watch yourself. And live joyfully. You are the master.' – Buddha

Divinely inspired by the fundamental, universal laws embedded in the core of Buddhism, these cards will help you foster an understanding of this ancient wisdom.

As you become familiar with the cards, you will find that this wisdom is not only practical and easy to access and cultivate, but you will notice that it brings peace, love and happiness into your life. Above all, the cards offer you a fun way to return to your true nature, the one you were born with, the Buddha nature – one that is open, joyful, pure, luminous, intelligent, and naturally kind and compassionate.

While navigating your way back to your true nature, you will travel the path of awakening. As you do so, you will learn to appreciate your and others' true beauty, elevate love and respect in all your relationships and be filled with peace and love for yourself and the world.

You will also find that you will more easily appraise your emotional and spiritual strengths and weaknesses, effortlessly dissolving negative thoughts and emotions as well as freeing yourself from mental limitations.

With your mind open and your heart tender, the Buddhism Reading Cards can help you on your path and bring you closer to your Buddha nature.

About The Cards

The *Buddhism Oracle* is designed as an easy and simple introduction to the fundamental teachings of Buddhism in a fun and practical way. Each card represents one fundamental, core principle of Buddhism.

The cards are simple to use, each containing a wisdom that, like a glimmer of light, brings healing, direction and inspiration to your life. The peaceful Buddha image helps the wisdom to flow easily, gently penetrating your mind and spirit.

By choosing the card that you most connect with, you can easily open up a way to positively communicate with your subconscious mind. You will find that the cards shine new light on situations by inviting inner solutions that come easily from the energy, creativity and intelligence found within your own, deep being.

Allow yourself the time and space to fully realise the meaning of the wisdoms and refer to the more detailed information in this book to help you go deeper in your understanding as you travel your path.

A basic understanding of Buddhism, meditation and mindfulness will help your understanding and ability to access the wisdom contained within the cards. By using the cards with an open and enthusiastic mind, you will naturally be drawn to increase your inner knowledge and awareness of this ancient wisdom.

The deck comprises 36 cards in total and is divided into four sections.

TRUTH CARDS

The truth cards draw on the Four Noble Truths – the four principles at the heart of the Buddha's teaching. They are based on the Buddha's philosophy that, 'There is suffering in the world and there are also ways to end suffering.'

These are your Truth Tools. They give you insight into your life's path. As you begin to see that conflict and struggle as well as dissatisfactions are part of the learning to release past pains, and transform misconceptions in the mind, you can then discover the path, freeing you from your own resistance and the battles within yourself.

By directly addressing the cause of your pain and unhappiness – on the material, emotional, psychological, or the most subtle, the spiritual level – each card illuminates the darkness within you, making an awakened heart possible in our ordinary living.

PURITY CARDS

Inspired by the Noble Eightfold Path and the skilful practices required to experience the moments of enlightenment in Buddhism, these cards reflect the eight major aspects of our lives that, by working through, can help bring about an end to our suffering.

These cards give you simple and easy-to-apply tools to purify your actions and unblock your vision so you can focus on your higher purpose. Like yoga or stretching exercises for the mind, if practised regularly, the chronic illnesses that are caused by the stiff mechanical gears in our mind can become well adjusted, allowing for a naturally healthy and happy state.

Contemplation cards

Structured around the Eight Fundamental Realisations in the dharma (the teaching of the Buddha), these cards are designed as medicinal tonics to gently eliminate the diseases of the mind. The Buddha recognised that these diseases of the mind are caused by our misconceptions, and are found in each one of us without exception.

These cards give you the wisdom to work in accordance with universal laws. Dharma will release you from the struggle of resisting reality as it is and from your own mental construct of illusion. Truth reveals itself to you; it is so simple. There will be no need to resist life once you have gained the insight and wisdom needed to live a natural and happy life.

Cultivation cards

These cards embody the sixteen fundamental virtues that have been highly recommended in order to cultivate a healthy human heart and mind in various Buddhism traditions through the ages. Each one of these virtues is used to conquer and eliminate deep-seated negative forces, like greed, anger, hatred, self-pity, jealousy and so on. Used daily for your own spiritual as well as physical benefit, practising these positive virtues will eliminate the negative and help build up your inner Buddha nature. Self-mastery begins with the cultivation of the intelligence of the heart. This process cannot be understood solely by the mind, however. Instead, like vitamins for our mind and spirit, cultivating these virtues will strengthen our mental faculties and show us the way to being a Buddha in the making, where your pure nature is peaceful, loving and happy.

Finally

Use the cards when you need direction, guidance, or in times of trouble. It can be easy to forget your own true Buddha nature in the midst of the busyness of life and the delusive clouds of discontentment but do not forget who you already are, and do not lose yourself in any fears.

Know also that these difficulties, conflicts and challenges happen to make the cultivation of your true

Buddha nature possible, so that a spiritual awakening becomes attainable on this path to enlightenment.

If you are grateful for these difficult times and practise your dharma well, your spirit will rise above all these troubles, reuniting with your own Buddha nature. Now, let this journey begin …

'On life's journey, faith is nourishment, virtuous deeds are a shelter, wisdom is the light by day and right mindfulness is the protection by night. If a man lives a pure life, nothing can destroy him.' – Buddha

How To Use The Cards

The *Buddhism Oracle* is healing, renewing and strengthening – and at its most powerful when you have the self-discipline to use it every day.

By using the cards daily – and acting on the wisdom contained within them – you will be empowered spiritually and strengthened mentally to take on life's challenges with ease and grace. By consciously contemplating the wisdom contained in one of the cards every day, you can heighten and purify your understanding of your own actions.

Regularly focusing on improving your spiritual, physical and emotional well-being can bring your life back into balance and, when used in this way, the cards can also become a powerful transformational tool, leading you to self-mastery.

Daily Mindfulness Practice

Early in the morning or before going to bed, prepare your question and, using your focused intention, draw a single card from the deck. Let your intuition guide you towards the Buddha's image on the front of the card that is right for you.

Select one card

Turn the card over and let yourself quietly contemplate the wisdom of the card. Reflect on the Buddha's wisdom as you consider your question. Take the time to get in touch with Buddha's one fundamental wisdom and apply it to one area of your life every day.

You can go even deeper by bringing the wisdom into your meditation practice. Simply sit in a quiet place, let your mind settle and be still. Focus on the Buddha wisdom on the card to help you see what is, clearly, and to release yourself from the attachment of any strong emotions or story.

Referring to the detailed wisdom pertinent to each card in this book will help you to understand the wisdom that you are working with even further. Consider the Reflections contained at the bottom of each page to fully reveal the wisdom within your own experiences and do the Actions suggested, to reveal the hidden truth.

Transformational Practice

This transformational practice works best when done on a weekly basis.

Simply divide the cards into four stacks in order according to their colour-coded sections. Be calm and focus. Let your intuition guide you towards the Buddha's image on the front of the card that is right for you and draw one card from each of the four stacks. Lay them out side by side.

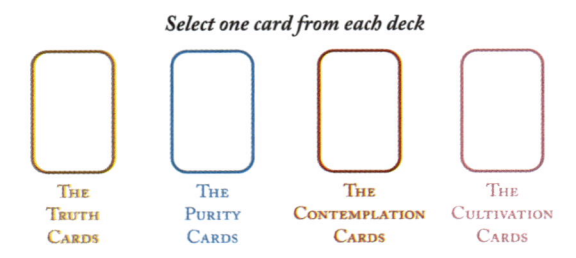

Select one card from each deck

| The Truth Cards | The Purity Cards | The Contemplation Cards | The Cultivation Cards |

Turn the cards over and use the Buddha's wisdom to reflect on your question. Be still in quiet contemplation.

Stand all four cards in a place where you can easily see them when rising in the morning and retiring from the day. When you see the cards, and throughout your day, be mindful to practise wise thoughts, wise feelings and wise actions according to the four cards that you have drawn. As you open up more and more to your own true Buddha nature, it will become easier to apply the wisdom to your own thoughts and actions.

Again, referring to the detailed wisdom pertinent to each card in this book will help you to understand the wisdom that you are working with even further. Considering the Reflections contained at the bottom of each page will help to fully reveal the wisdom within your own experiences and as you do the Actions suggested, the hidden truth will be revealed.

GOING FURTHER

As you become more familiar with the cards, you will begin to realise that your thoughts lead to actions, and your actions construct the world around you. There is a cause and effect system hidden in your trouble and conflict – and in your peace and happiness. Moreover, by using the Truth Cards to diagnose the origin of your problem, the cause and effect system behind your problem will reveal itself to you. Once you understand the root cause of your problem, the truth, you can use the Purity Cards to fine-tune your actions, the Contemplation Cards to strengthen your acceptance of the universal laws and then apply the Cultivation Cards to perfect your virtues.

Whichever way you use the cards, by getting in touch with their wisdom and practising mindfulness in your everyday life, you will soon see your own Buddha nature unfold as you walk this path to the heart.

'There are only two mistakes one can make along the road to truth; not going all the way and not starting.' – Buddha

Truth Cards
The Four Noble Truths

'Three things cannot be long hidden: the sun, the moon, and the truth.' – Buddha

The Truth Cards present the most fundamental of Buddha's teachings, the Four Noble Truths: suffering, the causes of suffering, the end of suffering and the path to end suffering.

Each of the Four Noble Truths set clear instructions for the actions and thinking needed to free us from this path of pain and suffering: understanding, letting go, realising and cultivating. These actions can turn human suffering into valuable lessons, freeing us to walk the path of enlightenment and live a fulfilling and wakeful life.

How To Work With The Truth Cards

To inquire about a painful feeling or emotion, simply draw a Truth Card, allowing yourself to connect with the Buddha's image that is most appealing to you.

By reading the insights, you can diagnose the root cause of your pain, and by doing the work needed you can understand, let go and release the pain and reveal the doorway to your own Buddha path.

To cultivate the truth, draw a card and consider the insight on the back of the card.

Refer to the detailed wisdom in this book specific to the card to go deeper and understand the universal truth. Reflect on the truth within your own experiences. Do the Action to reveal the hidden truth.

1. SUFFERING

THE FIRST NOBLE TRUTH

'There is a path leading to a complete deliverance from suffering.' – Buddha

Suffering is the feeling of extreme discomfort caused by an inability to fully accept things as they are. It applies to a range of human conditions like birth, illness, old age and death, as well as our own innate negative emotions and feelings.

Suffering can be experienced in many forms. Disappointment, rejection, unhappiness, loneliness and depression are all common forms of suffering. In fact, any feeling that causes us pain, distress or discomfort is really a form of suffering.

As human beings, we all want to experience more happiness and enjoyment in life. We have learned that the more pleasurable and joyful feelings we experience, the better. It therefore seems normal to want to avoid pain and struggle at all cost. And whenever difficulties do arise, it is common to feel something is wrong with us and try to cover it up as soon as possible. Buddha realised, however, that pain and suffering are simply transitory experiences – and none of these need be a permanent state of being. Once we understand that we experience suffering, we are not the suffering itself, we can expand our awareness into understanding the qualities and virtues within our sufferings and difficulties – and use this understanding to achieve peace and happiness. We do this by accepting that we have very little control over what happens to us, but that we do have control over how we respond to what has happened. We have control over what we say and how we feel and, most importantly, what actions we are better off taking to transform the situation. Once you awaken to this fundamental fact of life, you can transform any pain, conflict or struggle into a positive experience.

REFLECTION: Have you ever experienced great mental, emotional or physical pain?

ACTION: Find a way to turn this painful experience around and see the lesson hidden within.

2. Attachment

The Second Noble Truth

'Attachment to desire is the cause of suffering.' – Buddha

Attachment is an intense wanting to have something – a circumstance or even someone – which produces an extreme dissatisfaction with the way things currently are. When we want something different from what we are experiencing right here, right now, this unfulfilled desire causes us to experience discontentment. Worse, it disconnects us from the present moment – and the simple joy it contains.

Attachment can equally be caused by the strong desire not to have something. For example, feeling you won't be happy until you leave your job, end your relationship, move house, etc. But the harder you push something away, the more the feelings of attachment will cling to you.

These unfulfilled desires are the constant creations in your mind that separate you from the contentment of who you really are and what you are experiencing right now. It is important to realise that more, newer, better, or bigger is not going to fix everything in your life that you are currently not happy with. Instead, the pursuits of external sources of happiness only lead to more unfulfilled desires.

REFLECTION: Have you ever experienced problems or difficulties as a result of your strong emotional attachment to someone, something, or some circumstance?

ACTION: Write a list of the things that you currently want the most and become aware of how these attachments and desires affect your happiness and well-being.

3. Letting go

The Third Noble Truth

'Some of us think holding on makes us strong, but sometimes it is letting go.' – Herman Hesse

The Buddha's Third Noble Truth was that, in order to gain enlightenment, you have to consciously let go of all forms of suffering and delusions. Letting go is the conscious decision to detach yourself from the wants and desires of your mental, emotional and physical existence.

It means allowing things to simply be as they are, without the struggle or resistance that comes from trying to control an outcome or continually reminding yourself of an unhappy past event or negative emotion.

Many of us are carrying around enormously heavy burdens from experiences that happened in the past. Constantly reminding ourselves of unhappy events and circumstances that did not turn out how we wished drains an enormous amount of mental and emotional energy as we continuously relive and remind ourselves of these past events.

Letting go is the conscious decision to fully accept both your pleasant and unpleasant experiences without judgement. This allows you to remove the negative emotions from the memory of the experience, take the lessons contained within them, learn from them and move on.

Letting go is a conscious choice. You can choose to either let things go or let them be as they are. Choosing to let go is a powerful tool that can lighten the heaviness of the mind while allowing you to experience more joy and happiness in the present moment.

The mind obsesses while the heart is free. Letting go gives you the freedom to live joyfully from your heart in the present moment.

Reflection: Have you ever felt heaviness or unhappiness caused by replaying past events in your mind?

Action: Make a conscious choice to embrace and transform these memories in the past into a powerful lesson. Let go of the memories and learn the lesson.

4. The path

The Fourth Noble Truth

'No one saves us but ourselves. No one can and no one may. We ourselves must walk the path.' – Buddha

Buddha created the Noble Eightfold Path as a series of steps, or daily spiritual practices, that when followed can release us from suffering and attachments, leading us to greater happiness. (See the Purity Cards for a deeper explanation.)

Using these practical tools will enable you to create a different perspective. You will see things with a fresh eye and your new perspective will create the outcome that you heart is longing for. As you practise these processes and travel the path to self-actualisation, your dreams can become your reality.

The path is not a quick fix, however, and it won't provide you with an instantaneous answer to your difficulties, nor will conflicts just fade away. But if you are willing to practise the wisdom in the Purity Cards, your truth will be revealed.

Be aware also that the path to enlightenment is an endless process. You have to practise diligently and with discipline, but eventually, you will become the path itself, and fewer struggles and sufferings will come your way. Stay on the path, do the practices and process your experiences with this new perspective.

Awakening is not something to attain in the distant future but a way of living in the now; it is experienced moment by moment on the path.

REFLECTION: Are you feeling stuck with the same habitual thoughts, reactions and actions?

ACTION: List at least ten things you can do differently right now to create better feelings and outcomes.

PURITY CARDS
THE NOBLE EIGHTFOLD PATH

'Drop by drop is the water pot filled. Likewise, the wise man, gathering it little by little, fills himself with good.' – Buddha

The Purity Cards present the fundamental principles of the Noble Eightfold Path. These eight daily practices heighten the purity of your wisdom, as well as ethical actions and awareness. They set a course in wise actions for you to embrace your Buddha nature.

When your intention is pure, you can see truth as well as reality for what it is. The pathway will then be created for you to navigate into your spacious heart where peace, happiness and love are the foundation for all the solutions you are seeking to your challenges.

The Noble Eightfold Path lays out clear guidance for your daily practice to transcend your challenges in life no matter what the circumstances. This path of practice will gently take you back to experience inner freedom and enable you to love life again.

The more you practise these principles, the more your habitual impulse to react from a space of the ignoble and undignified will be diminished and the more awakening moments will flourish.

How To Work With The Purity Cards

To purify your actions, thinking, or intentions, simply draw a Purity Card. Let your inner knowingness connect to the Buddha image that is most appealing to you.

Quietly contemplate the wisdom on the card as it applies to you and your situation. To go deeper, refer to the card-related detailed wisdom in this book. Reflect on the truth within your own experiences and do the Action to reveal the hidden truth.

Use the Purity Cards daily to build your strength and create your own life. As you do, you will notice solutions appearing and challenges disappearing in the generous space you have created by your own practice. When your actions, thoughts and words are of a pure intention, they benefit your well-being and that of those around you.

To cultivate a noble character, draw a Purity Card each day for a month. Focus on embodying the wisdom of the card during the day and practise a noble act at every opportunity. Heighten your awareness of your actions, thoughts and feelings and purify your motivations and thoughts mentally, emotionally and spiritually.

At the end of the month, you will realise the power of your efforts and gain new wisdom in cultivating your noble character on this Buddha path.

5. Pure Understanding

The First Noble Eightfold Path

'The stillness of the heart reflects heaven on earth. As truth unfolds, with no strings attached, the heart becomes simple and pure.'
– Sofan

When there is confusion, you cannot clearly see what is happening to you or to the people around you. Strong emotions and judgements – either good or bad, right or wrong, gain or loss – have created a distorted view of what life is presenting to you. By practising pure understanding, you are required to take out the personal stories and fears created by the mind and strip away the toxic emotions of anger, self-doubt and frustration associated with what has happened. You are then asked to look at what has been happening, simply as what it is. You can then look at the same event but this time with the wise understanding of knowing exactly what happened to you and the people around you. A completely different perspective and insight may cause you to see new meanings. Confusion will be replaced with clarity. Frustration will be replaced with compassion. Self-pity will be replaced with certainty. When understanding is processed solely intellectually, logic is used as the basis for reasoning and the only important person to be considered most likely is you. This creates isolation and confusion.

Alternatively, you can look closely within yourself and take the understanding deep into your heart, allowing the positive forces of kindness, generosity and compassion to be part of the whole process. With a broadened perspective, your spacious heart and reasoning mind will take everyone's feelings and circumstances into account simultaneously, making a win–win situation the only acceptable outcome whereby everyone will benefit and be nurtured.

REFLECTION: Have you ever felt that even though you fully understand something intellectually, you still experience confusion?

ACTION: Write down a personal story that pains you. Then use just one word to describe the emotion that caused you the pain and release the painful emotion. Can you see the simple truth after the emotion has gone?

6. Pure Thought

The Second Noble Eightfold path

'We are shaped by our thoughts: we become what we think. When the mind is pure, joy follows like a shadow that never leaves.'
– Buddha

When we are free and living in purity of thought, we will not impose shoulds or should nots onto the world, onto someone else, or onto any situation. Whenever we speak of what should or shouldn't be, we are in denial of reality. In fact, we are trying to change reality in accordance with our expectations.

When practising purity of thought, you are asked to investigate your thoughts that don't lead to happiness, and to find out what motivates these thoughts. This practise requires you to look deep into your heart and question your own truthfulness in order to remove your own personal fantasy stories.

Only then will you simply embrace reality as what it is and see what has happened as for the best. You will stop struggling against reality and experiencing frustration and delusion. You can simply be yourself – loving, kind and fearlessly accepting of what life presents to you.

As the truth of reality meets the purity of thought in your practice, you will discover that every moment in your life that is unfolding has something to teach you and that everyone who comes your way is there to assist you to learn a greater lesson. Life is both precise and precious.

Reflection: When frustration arises, what are you struggling against with yourself or with the world?

Action: Write a page of who you would be if you weren't imposing your own expectations on yourself or others.

7. Pure speech

The Third Noble Eightfold Path

'Happiness comes when your words are pure, bringing about kindness and benefit to yourself and others.' – Buddha

Do you know what kind of world you are shaping for yourself and the people around you?

Every day you use words that shape your world and announce your intentions and desires. When you use harsh language with yourself and the people around you, or you intentionally hurt or belittle yourself or other people, are you truly free in your speech? Or are you simply caught up in the commotion of anger, hatred and unworthiness?

The words you use are like seeds you have chosen to plant in the garden of your heart – and in the garden of the world. You have the power to destroy yourself and poison the world around you or, more importantly, you have the power to plant beautiful flowers.

When practising purity of speech, you are aware of the consequences that your speech will bring about and you are willing to take full responsibility to create pure and kind words that benefit you and other people. You have the courage to examine the motivations behind your speech by asking – Is it true? Is it inspiring? Is it helpful? Is it kind? Is it necessary?'

Knowing your motivation behind your speech and reflecting before you speak are the main daily practices of purity of speech. These practices will free you as you use words that are truthful, kind and conducive to harmony, which in turn brings you peace and happiness and builds a better world.

REFLECTION: Have you ever regretted what you said?

ACTION: Write a positive letter that brings joy and love to a friend and watch the positive changes that unfold.

8. Pure action

The Fourth Noble Eightfold Path

'Refrain from that which is unskilful or that which harms. Do good and purify your heart. That is it.' – Buddha.

As you are constantly reacting to the busyness of the outside world, your mind will not be able to ask insightful questions about where you are going or how to live a life that is in tune with your higher purpose.

Instead, when practising purity of action, you are asked to consciously bring your inner awareness to your actions and by doing so, not to harm or destroy any life, not to take away things that don't belong to you and not to use sex in a harmful way to yourself or others.

The more you are able to practise purifying your own actions, the more your actions will be free from old habits, past experiences or any negative emotions. You will also be able to deepen your connection to your inner strength and rise above selfish motivations that only serve to benefit yourself.

With further practise, your daily actions will be encouraging and inspiring to others. When kindness and happiness are the basis of your actions, you enrich the lives of all those around you. Your actions become a pure celebration of our interconnectedness and when filled with loving-kindness, compassion and generosity, great changes can be made for a better world.

REFLECTION: Have your actions ever brought unhappiness or harm to others?

ACTION: Act with kindness and compassion to the people around you and bring joyful transformation to them.

9. Pure Livelihood

The Fifth Noble Eightfold Path

'Your work is to discover your world – and then with all your heart, give yourself to it.' – Buddha

Inside each of us, there is a longing to do work that helps others experience greater happiness and joy, work that builds a better world.

Everyone dreams of finding the perfect, well-paid job that provides a secure future and assumes that this secure future will bring happiness. But how many people have found this to be true? None.

Instead, are you able to make a conscious choice to follow your heart's longing and make a living by doing something that you love, regardless of how difficult it is to manage the fear and insecurity associated with an unknown future?

By practising purity of livelihood, you will consciously choose not to harm others in your work environment and will endeavour to find inner joy and job satisfaction in your employment. Know that the love you put into your work will inspire personal growth.

Ultimately, as you continue to practise, you will create a livelihood that allows you to assist other people's happiness and well-being as well as your own. Your strong work ethics alone provide you with the courage to walk into uncharted territory with certainty, regardless of others' disapproval and rejection and, in doing so, remain true to yourself.

When you are living your life's purpose, working with pure intention and a heightened awareness that is true to yourself, you will wake with vigour and inspiration every morning, enthusiastically ready to serve the world with your special gifts and talents.

REFLECTION: Are you able to give your heart and soul completely to your work?

ACTION: Write a list of all your special skills and talents and the ways they can serve the world.

10. Pure Effort

The Sixth Noble Eightfold Path

'Enlightenment is not your birthright. Those who succeed do so only through proper effort.' – Ramana Maharshi

Many spiritual masters were inspired to walk the Buddha path because they saw how the Buddha understood the mind and freed his heart from all kinds of human suffering.

Purity of effort refers to the mental effort required to understand the nature of this world in relation to your own life experience. Moreover, you are encouraged to practise daily – diligently and with discipline.

Your conscious effort, indomitable inner strength and unshakeable commitment will bring about lightness when encountering darkness, hope when experiencing self-doubt or disappointment, love when faced with hatred and joy instead of sadness.

This emphasis on maintaining your daily practice is central to all spiritual practices that bring about personal transformation and will enable you to be aware and awake to each moment in terms of how you live your life and this pure, constant effort leads to self-mastery.

REFLECTION: Have you ever forced something to happen in an unskilful way for your own benefit and caused unhappiness to others?

ACTION: Write down a list of the areas of your life where you have applied your skilful effort and it has benefited yourself and others.

11. Pure Mindfulness

The Seventh Noble Eightfold Path

'Mindfulness is the miracle by which we master and restore ourselves.' – Thich Nhat Hanh

Mindfulness is the most important thing we can do to regain our true well-being and happiness.

The mind has a tendency to go wandering in the past and venturing into the future. Very rarely does it takes any notice of what is happening in the present, thereby missing the most precious moments life has to offer.

Mindfulness practices, like meditation, yoga, art, music, as well as the martial arts, bring the awareness that what has happened in the past is only memory, and that what is going to happen in the future is a form of fantasy, while all opportunities and blessings unfold in the now.

Mindfulness keeps the mind still and clear, allowing the heart to open. In this state, we are able to experience clear insight – the ability to see things as they are, without judgement or prejudice.

The trained mind is anchored in the moment and understands that true happiness can only be experienced in the here and now. Knowing this can bring deep inner peace and empowerment as you realise that in the now, you have the power to change everything.

REFLECTION: Have you ever noticed that your mind loves wandering to the past and into the future?

ACTION: Write down a list of the feelings you have experienced when your mind is in the present moment either during meditation or when practising mindfulness.

12. PURE CONCENTRATION

THE EIGHTH NOBLE EIGHTFOLD PATH

'Thought is energy. Active thought is active energy. Concentrated thought is concentrated energy. Thought concentrated on a definite purpose becomes power.' – Charles Haanel

Concentration is the super-refined focus needed to notice what the mind is doing. When you have mastered this practice, no matter how easily your mind is distracted by your inner dialogue, the memories of the past, or the fantasies of the future, you are able bring it back to the present moment. You will be consciously focusing on where your mind is in relation to reality.

When you are deeply connected to the present moment, the forces of fear, anger or greed will stop pulling you off balance, causing you to experience pain and suffering. By allowing these negative forces to come and then pass through you without believing they are you, you will experience the awareness that comes from honouring this rising and falling of things without being caught in the downward spiral of destructive emotions.

True concentration will allow you to focus your mind perfectly in the present. In this way, your mind and body will gradually become calm and relaxed. There is a deep inner knowing that comes from understanding that you have the power to bring yourself back to the calm centre where love resides. This deep love is like a laser beam. It can penetrate all illusions of the outside world as well as the delusions of the inner world.

As you master your own mind, you will become more engaged with what you are working on and with the people around you.

Reflection: Have you ever been distracted by your inner dialogue, even when in a quiet and peaceful place?

Action: Find a quiet place and write down your inner dialogue. Is it relevant to who you are in the now?

Contemplation Cards

The Eight Realisations

'We are what we think. All that we are arises with our thoughts. With our thoughts we make the world.' – Buddha

The Contemplation Cards present the Eight Fundamental Realisations in the dharma. These are the essential ingredients that can turn your difficult experiences into rich wisdom, releasing you from struggles with reality and from your own illusory mental constructs.

Life is a series of self-realisations on the path to liberation. In this way, you expand and gradually change your thinking, ultimately removing all mental blocks and reuniting with the reality that you live in. Your connection to these universal truths will open up your own inner knowingness to the answer to any adversity.

Each of the Contemplation Cards gives clear insights for consideration and offers pathways for resolutions to be revealed.

How To Work With The Contemplation Cards

To remove mental blocks and reflect on life's essence, simply draw a Contemplation Card. Let your inner knowingness connect to the Buddha image that is most appealing to you.

Quietly contemplate the wisdom on the card as it pertains to your difficult experiences, removing any mental blocks as you do so. Resolutions will be revealed within you.

To go deeper, refer to the card-related detailed wisdom in this book. Reflect on the truth within your own experiences and do the Action to reveal the hidden truth.

To remove a major life trauma, draw a card daily. Deeply contemplate the wisdom on the card during your meditation practice until you truly realise the law of the universe.

In this contemplation practice the misconceptions of the mind will soon dissolve and negative emotions will be released as you re-establish your connection to your own Buddha nature.

To go deeper, refer to the card-related detailed wisdom in this book. Reflect on the truth within your own experiences and do the Action to reveal the hidden truth.

13. Impermanence

The First Realisation

'Thanks to impermanence, everything is possible.'
– Thich Nhat Hanh

It is our mind's habit to look for permanence in all things, but in reality, the natural law of the universe is built upon an undeniable impermanence – everything changes and everyone will experience the constant flux of life.

It is this tendency to form habits that makes us want to resist change, creating negative emotions and feelings towards the impermanent nature of human life and the ever-changing nature of this physical world.

When you understand this natural law of birth and death – where everything that rises must fall – you will gain a new perspective on your resistance to change. When you accept that you and everything in your life is constantly changing – and is supposed to – you will relax into your true nature.

This experience will bring a new insight into the ever-changing yet beautiful dance of nature and a renewed enthusiasm for new beginnings, renewing your faith and hope and making every moment precious.

Reflection: Have you ever felt stagnant and lifeless doing the same routine every day?

Action: Write a list of your old habits and fixed attitudes next to a list of the new habits you would love to create and the new moods you want to experience.

14. Awareness

The Second Realisation

'Awareness is like the sun. When it shines on things, they are transformed.'
– Thich Nhat Hanh

Awareness is the extraordinarily fine knowingness that comes from divinely combining the intelligence of the mind with the opening of the heart and the sensations of the body.

Each of these qualities is very different – feelings and emotions run like an electrical current through our physical body and we feel things that the mind can't understand.

The mind is constant evaluating – good or bad, right or wrong – and there is an instantaneous like or dislike of all things based on our past experiences.

Conversely, the spirit provides a certain inner knowingness that rises above both the duality structure of the mind and the pleasure and pain of the body.

But by opening the heart, wisdom can be gleaned from every internal and external event as acceptance is brought to the duality of life – good and bad, right and wrong, gain and loss, praise and blame.

Simply acknowledging these different layers of awareness will enable you to access a deeper understanding of reality. As you are intuitively drawn to or away from certain things, people or events on each level, you can create greater contentment and a greater sense of well-being.

Be steadfast on this spiritual path to enlightenment and strive to balance all three qualities. When they are simultaneously in sync with your truth, your own personal growth will be easily and naturally supported.

Reflection: What is your own definition of watching, observing and being aware?

Action: Find a quiet place and sit down comfortably with your eyes closed. Count how many different types of inner feelings and sensations come alive.

15. Desires

The Third Realisation

'The root of all suffering is desire.' – Buddha

Are we not all striving for a better tomorrow?

This single word, better, creates an unending stream of desires in the mind – and only serves for you to experience discontentment in the present moment, as these desires will never be fulfilled completely.

Instead, they only draw you into the fantasy of the future and away from the beauty of the present moment.

They are the natural product of the wanting mind – a mind that is always searching for something better or someone more perfect in order to ensure your survival – but wanting someone or something to be other than what it is in the now only takes you away from the appreciation of what you have and what life is offering to you now.

When you understand this, you are free to wisely choose not to be upset if your desires are not fulfilled. You can break free to connect with your heart, filling the present moment with gratitude and appreciation for how perfect your life truly is.

Reflection: Do you have any long-forgotten desires that were once significant and now have no value to you? What has changed?

Action: Write a list of your top ten desires. Once finished, cross out the bottom five and see how you feel.

16. Discipline

The Fourth Realisation

'A disciplined mind leads to happiness. An undisciplined mind leads to suffering.' – Dalai Lama

Discipline is one of the most-used, practical tools to reunite the mind, body and heart, and is encouraged in many spiritual pursuits as a way to attain ultimate happiness.

When you are disciplined, you come to know that you have the inner strength to persist with something until the journey ends. This is one of the most valuable tools you can use when trying to achieve a goal.

When you hear your inner voice saying it is too hard, unfair or disappointing, you know that you can rely on your commitment and patience to get back to your goal again.

This high level of commitment, fuelled by determination and patience, is rewarded by the fruitful outcome at the end – and self-trust and courage are established.

In this way, the practice of discipline upon the path can be more rewarding than even achieving the goal itself as you become the master of your own mind and embark on the journey to enlightenment.

REFLECTION: In which area of your life do you have the strongest discipline?

ACTION: Write down all the benefits you have experienced from being unshakeably disciplined.

17. Dharma

The Fifth Realisation

'Dharma can only be learned by direct experience. It educates the heart and liberates the mind.' – Sofan

Dharma is a heart and mind system of learning.

With your heart open, you become aware of the universal truths within your struggles and sufferings. You also come to understand that you have the power to turn these experiences around, knowing that there is a divine purpose unfolding.

The intelligence of the heart can see beyond the value system of the mind. By contemplating the universal truths and applying them to your own experiences, your heart will clearly understand the reality around you and purify your perceptions. As a result, you will be able to love the world as it is.

In the realisation of the dharma, there are always lessons to be learned. You become the faith student as you strive to understand the rises and falls that have made up your precious life.

By seeing the truth in dharma, your heart becomes wiser, kinder and more loving towards the world and especially yourself. Peace radiates from within you.

Reflection: Do you learn more in times of difficulty or when life is easy?

Action: Contemplate the possibility of becoming an eager, fresh student in every event in your life.

18. Forgiveness

The Sixth Realisation

'Holding on to anger is like grasping a hot coal with the intent of throwing it at someone else; you are the one who gets burned.' – *Buddha*

When love and compassion come together in the sacred space of the heart, they are released as the powerful energy of forgiveness. By practising forgiveness, you can find new meaning even in life's worst events.

Forgiving others helps you learn that we all need to be treated with kindness and respect. We all have fears and dreams, and experience confusion and frustration. We all have goodness in our hearts, too.

When you are able to forgive, in some significant ways everything begins to change, as all possibilities again become open to you.

This realisation allows you to go beyond the experiences that have triggered the anger and hatred in you. As you skilfully turn inward and seek the mystery of love and compassion in your heart, you begin to heal the pain from past betrayals, bringing a wholeness and balance to your life.

As you release this anger toward others, you will be freed from the resentment caused by any wrongdoing committed by others or yourself. Once this pain is released, it is possible for the heart to become open, making clarity of understanding and sustainable peace attainable in the here and now.

On a greater scale, when you are peaceful, the world around you will be peaceful. The forces of anger and hatred will be unable to penetrate your space and you truly will be helping heal the wounds of the world.

REFLECTION: Has your refusal to forgive ever led to you experiencing destructive emotions?

ACTION: Write a list of people, events and your own wrongdoings that you are ready to forgive right now.

19. Detachment

The Seventh Realisation

'Manifest plainness. Embrace simplicity. Reduce selfishness. Have few desires.' – Lao Tzu

Detachment allows you to be liberated from the natural tendency of the mind to want more of everything – more love, more food, more space, or even more accomplishments and achievements. It allows you to not get caught up in the negative emotions associated with any of these unfulfilled desires of the mind.

By practising detachment as a spiritual contemplation tool every day, you investigate all the basic human wants and desires deeply. You know how to distance yourself from the wanting and the desires as well as the clingy emotions towards these desires and know not to identify yourself as those desires.

In this realisation, you learn how to detach from the outcome and hold the pure intention to enjoy the process of whatever you are doing in the now. Furthermore, your detachment from planning well into the future will enable you to welcome every day as new and exciting and let unimaginable opportunities flow freely into your life.

Ultimately, this practice of detachment is like an invisible surgical scalpel – it has the spiritual power to remove and cut away destructive emotions in the mind, the clinging of the pleasurable sensations in the physical body, and certain harmful addictions, permanently.

REFLECTION: Consider a major positive change from your past that arose when you detached from old habits in order to adapt to a new situation.

ACTION: Write a list of destructive emotions and harmful addictions that you want to detach from and investigate their karmic law in you.

20. KARMA

THE EIGHTH REALISATION

'The more you practise karma, the more you will discover that you are the master of your own fortune and the creator of your own destiny.' – Sofan

Karma is easy to understand – in the simplest Buddhist terms, karma means cause and effect. Good actions and generous thoughts bring about positive feelings and happy events. On the contrary, bad thoughts and ill actions will inevitably bring negative emotions and the unfolding of unfortunate events.

In the realisation of karma, you will not fall into the delusions of the mind. You will not believe that it is only luck when fortunate events come your way. Similarly, when sad events knock on your door, you will not feel unfortunate. You are granted the inquisitive insight to look deeper into the causes and effects as well as the actions and consequences.

When using karma as a contemplation tool for your spiritual advancement, it enables you to be strong and courageous and look deeper into your past actions and take full responsibility for life as it unfolds.

You fully realise that you have planted the karmic seeds in the past and they are germinating when both the external and internal conditions become possible in the present. Flowers or weeds, fortunate or unfortunate, they are all there with you.

When practising karma, you will be mindful to plant good thoughts and positive actions every day in your own life and with the people around you. Your thoughts and actions are powerful and are carrying tremendous energies. Like echoes, you can count on these energies returning to you without exception in the material, emotional and especially on the spiritual level.

REFLECTION: Can you see the karmic act unfolding in your life?

ACTION: Plant a positive seed with your actions today. Cultivate it with good intention and loving-kindness and see how long it takes to germinate.

CULTIVATION CARDS
THE SIXTEEN VIRTUES

'When you come upon a path that brings benefit and happiness to all, follow this course as the moon journeys through the stars.' – Buddha

The Cultivation Cards consist of sixteen virtues which are inspired by the Ten Perfections, the Seven Factors of Enlightenment and some other most valued virtues in Buddhism. These virtues are useful tools in cultivating the illumination of the mind and heart. When practised every day, you will find your mind, body and spirit working together harmoniously and in peace.

You will also discover that awakening is no longer something outside of you to be achieved in the distant future. Instead, it is a process whereby your own innate Buddha nature is slowly revealed through daily effort, concentration and focused awareness. Cultivate and nurture these virtues as you would a garden.

When you understand that these practices bring perfection, you become daring, free and fearless. You will be the dreamer who dreams awake and your dreams will become the reality that you live.

How To Work With The Cultivation Cards

To remove negative emotional forces and cultivate your Buddha nature, simply draw a Cultivation Card. Let your inner knowingness connect to the Buddha image that you are drawn to most strongly.

Quietly contemplate the wisdom on the card, cultivating the intelligence in the heart and growing your Buddha nature.

To go deeper, refer to the card-related detailed wisdom in this book. Reflect on the truth within your own experiences and do the Action to reveal the hidden truth.

This is most effective when done every day for a month. Focus on your mind's natural tendency to react to daily challenges and consider how you can resolve your challenges in luminous new ways.

21. SELF-ACCEPTANCE

THE FIRST VIRTUE

'To be beautiful means to be yourself. You don't need to be accepted by others. You need to accept yourself.'
– Thich Nhat Hanh

Once you accept who you are, you no longer need to struggle to become someone you are not. You are truly free to fully explore the talents and special gifts that you were born with – gifts and skills to be used in service for other people and the world. Your purpose in life can only flourish with your self-acceptance.

The cultivation of self-acceptance frees you to love who you truly are and forgive what you have done. It gives you the power to explore and attain your own full potential and wholeness. You then become your own saviour and healer of your own painful wounds.

In practising self-acceptance, you are called upon to open up and face your own vulnerability and to know it as your strength. You accept fear as part of your own making and develop courage from the heart to overcome any fear. In true acceptance of yourself, you honour your wounds as part of your journey to experience human fullness. You can reframe disappointment within a broadened outlook.

As you accept yourself for who you are, all self-judgements will fall away. You will gain the wisdom to see your shortcomings as special strengthening tools for self-improvement, your failures as valuable lessons, and your life as a precious gift from the divine.

Other people's judgement will have very little power over you since self-esteem, self-love, self-trust and all variations of the self will be brought to the light. Your unshakeable inner knowing of your true worth will be deeply grounded in human integrity.

REFLECTION: Do you have compassion for yourself or do you judge yourself harshly?

ACTION: Write a list of areas where you judge yourself mercilessly. Now write an action plan to bring about positive change in each area.

22. GENEROSITY

THE SECOND VIRTUE

'A true spiritual life is not possible without a generous heart.' – Buddha

Generosity refers to our ability to give and share what we have both freely and wholeheartedly.

This noble act is a heartfelt kindness in response to the intrinsic human need for love and affection. As you give with no strings attached, no expectations and no manipulations, your heart expands outwardly in compassion and loving-kindness for others.

True generosity is performed without any sense of loss or expectation of reward. It dissolves the fear of scarcity and separateness and frees the receiver from any negative emotional obligations. In this reciprocal arrangement, both the giver and the receiver enjoy the boundless generosity given from a spacious heart and appreciate the richness only attainable by mutual sharing.

Kindness and gratitude are the foundations for this noble act that deepens human bonding and the sense of oneness that it brings as it builds a greater community. As you cultivate generosity in your daily life, you will naturally find more and more opportunities to be so. It can be as simple as giving your full attention as you listen to a friend, offering a kind word to uplift the spirit of another or being patient with someone. Graciously, you will also become much more grateful for the generosity shown to you.

REFLECTION: Can you recall some instances when you were deeply touched and moved by another's generosity of spirit?

ACTION: Practise showing kindness to those around you today, either in action or in emotional support.

23. Compassion

The Third Virtue

'Our task must be to free ourselves from this prison by widening our circle of compassion to embrace all living creatures and the whole of its beauty.' – Albert Einstein

True compassion is the pure intention to release all pain and suffering. It is a unique, innate, constructive force. It wells up within us and connects with the pain and suffering of all living things.

Compassion enables you to forgive yourself, first and foremost, and your own wrongdoings as well as other disappointing events and people. By cultivating self-love and loving-kindness in your own being, and uncovering your own pains and sorrows, you are healed, too.

Where there is compassion, there is no my pain, your pain, their pain, or our pain – it is simply the pain of the universe in all of us and in all living things. When you feel it, there comes a calling to release it, like a mother naturally comforting her crying baby.

By relieving the suffering of others – even your enemies – it releases pain from within yourself, and others, and creates mutual happiness. It uplifts the human spirit and reveals our own true Buddha nature.

Being able to respond to pain, sorrow, worry and trouble with loving-kindness and compassion empowers you and the people around you to bring positive changes and happiness into the world.

With a trained, compassionate heart, you can see the innate goodness and potential in all living things, including yourself. This willingness to be vulnerable creates a powerful opening for the people around you to have compassion to heal their own pains, too.

REFLECTION: Do you have a big enough heart to forgive yourself and bring compassion to your life?

ACTION: Write down all the good reasons that you should forgive yourself.

24. COURAGE

THE FOURTH VIRTUE

'It is not the strength of the body that counts, but the strength of the spirit.'
– *J.R.R. Tolkien*

Courage is a spiritual strength that takes you beyond all fear and resistance. It gives you the insight to understand that external difficulties are merely the reflection of your unresolved internal resistance, and the knowledge that you have the inner fortitude to remove internal and external blockages on the path.

By practising courage, you will be grounded inwardly in certainty and peace until your whole being is radiating with the deepest inner strength, allowing you to take charge during times of difficulty. Resolutions will arise from your fearless state of mind and you will not allow negativity or other people to spin you out of your calm centre.

When you are in your own warrior spirit, secure in the knowledge that you have courage deeply centred within you, you dare to embrace every challenge in life and fear shifts to wonderment at what mysteries life will bring.

Reflection: Have you ever been frozen in fear and used wishful-thinking statements like, 'When I … then I will …' to delay actions?

Action: Take courage and turn your wishful thinking into a statement that leads to action such as, 'I am capable of … and now I am going to …'

25. Patience

The Fifth Virtue

'At the end of the way is freedom. Till then, patience.' – Buddha

Patience is a fine, noble quality that implies everything is possible in time and space.

A deep knowingness reminds you that nothing can fail you but your own impatience – there is no imperfection because you have the forbearance to ultimately achieve perfection.

When you are patient with yourself, you are in fact cultivating self-love. When you are patient with others, you are forging a pure intention to be kind and compassionate and your selfless aspiration will help them achieve their goals. Patience gives you the endurance to overcome frustration in the face of difficulty and the tenacity to achieve your goals. You can rest in the calmness of your mind and remain focused and committed. Every action motivated by patience builds meaning and purpose in your life.

Through patience, the linear quality of time becomes infinite and the limited physical space turns into the whole universe. By standing in this timeless universe firmly and patiently, you are unstoppable until your dreams come true.

REFLECTION: What internal resistance have you experienced when being patient?

ACTION: Choose one aspect of your life in which you are willing to apply patience daily until your goal is accomplished.

26. Gratitude

The Sixth Virtue

'If you want to turn your life around, try thankfulness. It will change your life mightily.' – Gerald Good

Gratitude is a powerful kindness energy.

It is expressed outwardly by giving thanks for the richness brought to you by other people, their services and contribution. Your gratitude builds a feeling of kinship among others, breaking down all barriers of separateness.

By practising gratitude, you will radiate positive feelings as you show your appreciation. Your kind, encouraging words will build bridges, connecting you with other people.

On a deeper level, this practice encourages you to respond with thankfulness to all aspects of your life – from love to nourishment, nature, shelter, friendship, education and the many other precious gifts that are given to you freely. You are able to reflect deeply and know how fortunate we truly are.

By cultivating gratitude, you expand beyond your own limited self and understand that we are all supporting and nurturing each other in the oneness of space. You have an inner knowing that the special skills and talents in each of us are there to assist us all in our growth.

The noble practice of gratitude will connect you to the fullness of all our lives and your own greatest potential.

REFLECTION: Can you give thanks to every part of your body that is working harmoniously to sustain your life?

ACTION: Write a list of your personal possessions that are provided, made, or created by others. See how much gratitude can be generated by your list.

27. Happiness

The Seventh Virtue

'The very purpose of our life is to seek happiness.' – *Dalai Lama*

Have you ever wondered why so many things that you seek do not bring about happiness?

As you will know from your own experiences, the pleasurable sensations sought after by the body and the achievements and successes chased after by the mind can only satisfy your desires temporarily until this elusive chase leaves you thoroughly exhausted.

The highest and purest state of happiness is of an independent nature. You can only experience it when the mind is quiet and the heart is open, and a pure connection is made with your own true self, other people and the world around you.

Happiness arises naturally when you live by your own true value. When your authentic self is truly living an authentic life, you are truly kind, compassionate, generous and truthful. You strive to serve others and help them achieve the same high value of happy living as you.

Happiness is not derived from that object, thing or person you are so longing for. It is only attainable by your sincere serving, giving, sharing and creating, and by embodying the values needed for our higher evolution.

REFLECTION: In this moment, what do you really want to feel?

ACTION: Create a list of activities that you love to do that will enhance feelings of happiness, authenticity and truthfulness.

28. Truthfulness

The Eighth Virtue

'Like a lovely flower, bright and fragrant are the fine and truthful words, of the man who says what he means.' – Buddha

Truthfulness reveals itself in the profoundness of simplicity.

Looking at a blooming flower, do we see truthfulness in it? The simple answer is yes. All that it is, is right in front of you. No more and no less. No exaggeration and no minimisation.

When we look at a wilting flower in the final stage before death arrives, do we see truthfulness in it? The answer is also yes. All that it is, is right in front of our eyes. There is no shame and no fear. No sorrow in the lost beauty. No guilt in the lost battle of forever-blooming youth. It is still standing proud in the midst of the beauty of all inspiring creations.

Truthfulness means that you show people who you really are without exaggeration, or a need to impress, or try to be something you are not. In this practice you are required to look deep within yourself and investigate what truth is for you. Truth is so often hidden behind your own opinions of things, of people and of the world.

When you drop the opinions, truth reveals itself.

Speaking and acting skilfully in accordance to your own true value is the ultimate form of truthfulness. By practising this perfection of truthfulness, your heart has the highest intention to preserve human integrity and dignity. Truth ultimately sets you free to live in accordance with the highest human values possible.

Reflection: Are you true to yourself? Consider why or why not.

Action: Write a list of things that you have the power to change and act on in order to live an authentic life.

29. Loving-kindness

The Ninth Virtue

'When we feel love and kindness toward others, it not only makes others feel loved and cared for, but it also helps us to develop inner happiness and peace.'
– Dalai Lama

Loving-kindness is an all-encompassing act. It is fuelled by our inner strength, unconditional love, compassion, forgiveness, patience and many other noble human traits.

Loving-kindness is the distilled essence of pure love. As you open your heart, you are able to love the unlovable, bring joy to sadness, faith to doubt and light to darkness. As you bring pain and sorrow into the light, feelings of anger, self-pity or even grief will gradually dissolve as you nurture them with your pure love.

In sharing and giving this loving-kindness, everyone regardless of what they have done, what pain and suffering they carry, what past and future they are holding, are all nurtured and replenished by your loving-kindness, yourself included.

By practising loving-kindness every day you raise consciousness of human integrity and dignity, and the more you cultivate loving-kindness towards yourself, the more you are able to help other people and the whole human race pursue happiness.

REFLECTION: In which areas of your life are you critical or judgemental of yourself?

ACTION: Using your answer to the question above, meditate and cultivate this loving-kindness mantra daily until the pain and fear disappears.

May I be filled with loving-kindness;

May I be safe from inner and outer dangers;

May I be well in body and mind;

May I be at ease and happy.

30. DETERMINATION

THE TENTH VIRTUE

'It is you who must make the effort. The master only points the way.' – Buddha

Determination embodies the mental quality of lasting endurance, the physical quality of healthy, vibrant earth energy and the spiritual quality that comes with knowing you are moving in the right direction.

When all three qualities are in harmonious equilibrium, you will move towards your goals swiftly, experiencing pure clarity in your heart and mind and cutting through all fear-based forces like indecision, hesitation, laziness or even withdrawal.

Great faith and strong willpower fuel your unwavering commitment to achieve worthwhile goals. The wisdom to be found in determination leads you to work on your tasks with great discipline and your inner strength means that unfavourable situations or other people's opinions will have no power over you. Nothing is unattainable when this noble quality of determination is cultivated.

On this path of practice there are no ends and no beginnings. Only the practice of determination will reveal to you that every life experience is one more opportunity for self-realisation as the universe unfolds the truth within you.

REFLECTION: By your own unwavering determination, what have you achieved?

ACTION: Identify how you would use determination to remove mental as well as external obstacles.

31. Equanimity

The Eleventh Virtue

'I find hope in the darkest of days, and focus in the brightest. I do not judge the universe.' – Dalai Lama

We experience different feelings – pleasure or pain, praise or blame, loss or gain – while moving through our daily life. This duality exists in our mental value system and is the automatic response of an untrained mind. It is common for us to experience this unstable nature as our mind spins while trying to understand these opposing forces.

With training, however, a calm mind can be created. This enables you to realise these opposites are actually the same thing. The true reality is hidden within your own inner peace. By cultivating equanimity, you can rise above these dualities, and experience pain without complaining. If you look deeper into the pain, you will come to see it as a valuable lesson to be learned so that you can take the appropriate wise actions to release the pain and return to your own true nature. In practising this perfection of equanimity, you forge an unshakeable courage to experience all circumstances that come your way, without judging them as good or bad, right or wrong, gain or loss, so that you are no longer disturbed by your own negative emotions. Nothing then can spin you out of your calm centre.

Your cultivation of equanimity will ultimately expand your capacity to taste the sweetness in the bitterness and seek the spark of spirit in amongst our humanness.

Reflection: Have you ever been upset by an unfortunate life event but later considered it a blessing?

Action: Write out a sad life event that happened in the past. Now, use your insight to rewrite it as a happy event.

32. Wisdom

The Twelfth Virtue

'Know well what leads you forward and what holds you back, and choose the path that leads to wisdom.'
– Buddha

Buddha taught that wisdom is the actual means by which we purify ourselves. Just knowing this brings calmness, then faith, and eventually truth.

To cultivate wisdom, the mind is trained to become quiet amidst the changing nature of all things, including external stimulants and inner dialogue. This stillness connects us to the natural laws of the universe, expands our awareness and leads us back to the sacredness inside, where peace overcomes fear.

Meditation is one of the easiest and most profound ways to get in touch with your inner wisdom. Yoga, walking in nature, art, music – in fact, doing anything you love – are all effective ways of reaching this inner wisdom.

Wisdom comes when the heart understands what the mind can't fathom. You will discover a supreme clarity, seeing things as they truly are and acting with integrity as your impeccable words and actions lead you to overcome life's challenges effortlessly.

REFLECTION: Have you ever experienced a strong calling to act on something that didn't make sense at the time but eventually led you to an extraordinary experience?

ACTION: Write down three aspects of your life in which you are feeling stuck. Now use the wisdom you have gained to find a solution for them.

33. Peace

The Thirteenth Virtue

'Compassion, forgiveness, these are the real ultimate sources of power for peace and success in life.'
– Dalai Lama

Peace cannot be experienced while your mind is busy thinking ahead or reliving past memories. Instead, you are required to quiet the mind and experience your inner feelings honestly without judgement, like when you meet with a dear friend. Your true nature of peace, love and happiness, which was once hidden by the dense crowd of thoughts, will then be revealed to you.

You also need the courage to become vulnerable so that your heart can become soft, tender and open. When you are willing to sit with your true feelings, practise loving-kindness for others, compassion for the world and self-love, peace can be attained within you.

Buddha said that, 'Tranquility of mind comes from having successfully transcended greed, hatred and ignorance.' Therefore, to cultivate peace and the profound, the universal wisdom within you has to rise above greed to practise generosity wisely, transform hatred into acceptance and anger into loving-kindness. As you consciously choose to transcend these delusive forces within you, you will experience profound inner peace.

REFLECTION: In which areas of your life do you experience most inner peace? How so?

ACTION: How could you expand that feeling of inner peace into the areas of your life where you experience fear and self-doubt?

34. UNCONDITIONAL LOVE

THE FOURTEENTH VIRTUE

'To love means to cherish, to be compassionate, to be of service, to be tolerant and to be wise.' – Venerable Master Hsing Yun

Unconditional love is a free-flowing, positive energy. You can only feel this love by expressing it, and the more you give your love unconditionally the more your heart is able to connect with this pure, nurturing, universal force.

The concept of unconditional love implies you are giving it freely, that is, without negative feelings or emotions towards anyone, yourself, or the world. When your action is purely motivated by unconditional love, everything and everyone becomes fully alive, fully conscious of their highest potential and human integrity.

This practice is the foundation for all other cultivations of patience, loving-kindness, generosity, courage, determination, gratitude and freedom. This positive force alone can transcend the lower forces like selfishness, greed, anger and many other forms of human suffering.

Your willingness to cultivate unconditional love will nurture and cure the wounded physical bodies, spirits and the wounds of the world, so that the well-being in you and in the world around you will be restored to perfect balance.

Unconditional love is expansive and provides you with the insight to see goodness in all living things and your own life experiences. It connects you to the highest purpose of what being human truly means – to love and connect with one another freely and purely.

Reflection: Have you ever been touched by unconditional love so profoundly that you were able to change your life path for the better?

Action: Apply unconditional love to an area of your life in which you feel frustrated. Notice the change it makes.

35. RENUNCIATION

THE FIFTEENTH VIRTUE

'Give up all ideas about yourself and simply be.' – Nisargadatta Maharaj

There is a great difference between struggling in life and loving life.

When we struggle, we are often trying to hold on to something we should no longer have at any cost. The practice of renunciation, or voluntarily letting go, will help you end this struggle and make loving life possible. For when you are not struggling, you can give all you have to love, to dream, to be who you truly are and do everything that you do wholeheartedly.

Daily practise in this virtue can come in many different forms, but all help remove blockages, which create openings for growth and consciousness expansion. One of the easiest practices to begin with is to literally let go of your unwanted possessions.

However, to go further in this practice, you must also let go of all the struggles that are dragging you down, like your destructive relationships, your addictions, as well as any self-pity, lack of self-worth, hatred and anger towards yourself and others. By removing internal struggles, you will be able to overcome external obstacles.

Renunciation is not about giving up, rather it is about giving your whole self to your true nature. When you are willing to let go, you can change anger into peace, manipulation into pure love, a secure home into a wild adventure and the need to be right into true, loving relationships. Most of all, you can let go of the need for a certain outcome and embrace the magnificent, continuous process of being wild and free.

REFLECTION: How many old undesirable habits and emotions can you let go of?

ACTION: Make a list of exciting new habits you want to replace the old ones with.

36. Energy

The Sixteenth Virtue

'You are never alone or helpless. The force that guides the stars guides you too.' – Shrii Shirr Anandamurti

The cultivation of energy is more than just boundless, physical energy – it is about making a divine connection with the universal life force that motivates all creations in the universe and in you.

This inspiring energy enables you to stand strong and tall in the midst of difficult circumstances with a deep knowing that they will soon pass. This noble energy illuminates the heart and mind. As your inner light shines clearly, you are able to see reality for what it is and you are set free from the delusions of the mind, which are full of doubts and fears.

The more you cultivate this noble energy, the more you will be able to enlighten every ordinary moment and fill it with creative life forces as you are guided by the divine wisdoms and empowered by higher forces. You will soon realise that the beauty in the mystery of life is unfolding in front of your very eyes.

You can cultivate this universal energy by meditating in silence and going within to a deep space of refuge, rest and strength, reconnecting fully with love, forgiveness and profound healing. This spiritual connection with the universal and wholesome force empowers you to become fearless.

REFLECTION: Have you ever been guided by divine forces and felt infallible?

ACTION: Find some quiet time to do the meditation practice and connect to your inner life force.

About ...
Buddha

Born Prince Siddhartha in a little kingdom where Nepal is today, Gautama Buddha grew up in tremendous luxury in royal palaces about 2,600 years ago. It had been prophesied that he would one day become a great, spiritual teacher or a great compassionate king. His father, the king, naturally wanted to him to become a great king and tried to confine the prince inside the beautiful palaces so he would never see any kind of suffering or distress in the real world. Indeed, until he was twenty-nine, around him there were only beautiful people and things. He never saw old age or sickness, ugliness or death. He went on to live an opulent, royal life with his wife Yasodhara and son Rahula. His curiosity about the real world, however, finally led him to wander out of the palace to make his own good fortune. As he did, the prince Siddhartha encountered a senile old man, a sick man, a corpse on its way to the funeral and an ascetic. He truly was in the real world – for the first time. After seeing all this suffering, Siddhartha thought his life of material comfort and refined beauty had been a waste. He became an ascetic, too, seeking to discover what there was beyond sickness, old age and death, poverty and pain. Seeing the suffering in the world was the beginning of the Buddha's quest to find a cure for healing the human condition, and led him on the path of enlightenment, which he attained after six years of contemplation and meditation. When he awoke from his meditation, people asked:

'What are you? Are you a god?'

'No,' replied the Buddha.

'Are you an angel?'

'No.'

'Then, what are you?' they asked.

'I AM AWAKE,' he replied.

His quest transformed him from the royal prince Siddhartha to Buddha – one of the greatest spiritual teachers throughout the ages – and his father, wife and son all became his disciples. Buddha tirelessly travelled and taught dharma after his enlightenment until his death at age eighty. In his teaching, he stated, 'If it were not possible to embody peace and freedom and compassion, I would not teach you to do so. But because it is possible, I offer these wisdoms for you.'

YOUR BUDDHA NATURE

As you begin to play with the *Buddhism Oracle* you will start to develop an awareness of the beauty within your true nature and intuition. By choosing the Buddha image on the card that you most connect with you are, in fact, trusting the intelligence of your heart, safe in the knowledge that the true answer lies within you. As you develop in self-realisation and dare to show the world who you really are, the true answer to your problem will emerge from the depth of your being – a place that is naturally pure, full of wisdom and love. Buddha never put much emphasis on belief alone. Instead, he encouraged us to try and understand the reality of our own being and how our mind works. He never insisted that we had to learn what he was, what a Buddha is. All he wanted was for us to understand our own nature.

In fact, Buddha saw himself as a human being like all of us, as well as a teacher. Moreover, he strongly believed that every man and woman can become a Buddha by applying similar wise thinking and effort. The Buddha's wisdom therefore encourages you to believe something is true because you have seen how it works and have observed that very thing within yourself – your truth comes from your own life experiences. And the more you allow the intelligence of your heart to flow softly into every aspect of your life, the more you will experience your own Buddha nature – one that is interconnected with the universal wisdom of love, peace and happiness.

Mindfulness

Mindfulness training is a way of checking in with your mind, your thoughts, feelings, sensations and emotions – and understanding that you are not these unceasing activities. It is as simple as pausing for a moment and concentrating the mind. Focus your energy and direction on the present moment. If you feel anger, depression or stress, try not to identify yourself as angry, depressed or stressed. Instead, recognise that these feeling are merely energies that come and go. Accept each and every one of these energies without judgement and let them go. You can imagine them drifting off on the wings of a bird, or as a leaf falls from a tree, or as the water runs out with the tide.

As you detach from identifying with these emotions – and practise letting these and the many other emotions, bodily sensations and thousands of thoughts you have in a day go – you can consciously reconnect with the sacredness of life.

A simple and easy way to practise mindfulness daily

As you recentre yourself in the present moment, this place of stillness can help you reconnect with the presence of your own heart and develop insight and clarity about your true reality. Try the following daily. Take a moment and have a break from all mental, physical and emotional activities.

Step one: Stop

Take a moment and have a break from all mental, physical and emotional activities.

Step two: Take a deep breath

Breathe into your calm centre and recentre yourself.

Step three: Observe

Pay attention to what is happening inside you, including all your thoughts, emotions and sensations. In the stillness of the present moment, reconnect with your sacred self.

Step four: Proceed

Firmly connect with the greater intelligence of your heart and your sacred self. There is no need to judge, analyse or figure out what is right or what is going wrong. Just allow yourself to be in the here and now, knowing who you are and also what you are not. Calmly reorganise your thoughts, feelings and emotions in accordance with your very own experience of the moment.

A final thought

Mindfulness is a powerful practice that will allow you to make a major shift from being a doer to becoming an observer. By being an observer of what is happening, you can make a conscious choice to do, think and feel with more peace, balance and purpose.

Meditation

Meditation is an integral part of mindfulness training in Buddhism. The idea is to simply quiet the mind and create an opening where we can feel the tenderness of the heart. It is an invitation to see the world as it is, in the presence of your sacred self, as your heart opens. There is no right way or wrong way to practise meditation. It is a personal experience of the peace within yourself in the meditative state. Self-discipline is essential for daily meditation practise. At the beginning, five to ten minutes of practise in the morning or before bed is enough.

As you practise more regularly, you will know the perfect length of time for your own practice that allows you to experience your own sacred self – one that is pure and full of love, happiness and peace.

A DAILY MEDITATION PRACTICE

This practice is as easy as sitting comfortably in a chair in a quiet place with your palms open and receptive, resting on the top of your knees.

Make sure your spine is straight and upright with dignity. Gently close your eyes. Now, in a relaxed manner, take a long, deep breath in. Simply be aware that you are breathing in.

At ease, take a long deep breath out and just notice that you are breathing out. Keep following the deep breath in, and naturally letting the deep breath out. When thoughts come and go in your mind, just be aware of the movement of your thoughts. Know that you are not your thoughts.

As you become aware of feelings and sensations in the body, know that you are not these physical feelings or sensations of the body.

As you notice streams of subtle emotions flowing through the emotional body (such as stress, resistance, defensiveness, anxiety, fear, tiredness or excitement), know that you are not these emotions.

Instead, you are the observer of the mind, of your thoughts, feelings, sensations and emotions during the meditation. Observe every moment as it comes and pay attention to the tenderness of the heart. By simply observing and realising the presence of the heart in every moment that the mind is still, you are cultivating kindness and compassion of the heart.

The Author And Artist: Sofan Chan

Exotic East is where I was from, growing up in the chaotic Hong Kong of over seven millions earthlings. My playgrounds were the temples, wet-markets, crowded streets and jungly back hills behind the concrete highrises. It helped me to develop some of my superpowers - to create toys with my wild imagination for amusement when there was none within my reach, to turn chaos into order, difficulties into peace, dwelling in the inner silence to soften the external symphonies of noises.

After leaving my home country, where I worked as an interior designer, I went to study art in the Art Institute of Chicago before then moving to Australia, where I graduated with a Masters in Applied Buddhist Studies.

Falling in love with the Australian spacious wilderness and a wild Australian man led me to a couple years well spent on one long road trip circumferencing this precious land and to live like Henry Thoreau in the Walden Pond, a simple cottage with no electricity, no running water, no flushing toilet; in a word, no comforts of the modern world for another few years. This experience helped me to acquire my superpowers in growing my own vegetables, flowers and fruit trees; tending my horses and riding to town rather than driving the car; living simply with what I had rather than going to the shop; loving my own company and creating art to bring out my inner essence in the wilderness.

Once I finished my initiation to the wild Australian lifestyle I moved back to Sydney. Here I have been living on a small island where a serene river meets the powerful sea in the early 2000s and have been working on the wildest pursuits in my art. Detours were many, being a mother of three incredible human beings, renovating a country pub. This list is long and weary; nonetheless these lived experiences of hopes and dreams, drama and dharma, victories and defeats, adventures and adversities contribute to who I am today. As the mind never stops creating roadblocks on the way, watching myself tumble and fall, getting up and going again, many tears shed and much laughter shared; because of the ONE dream which I can't ignore as it originated from the heart; so here I go again.

You can find out more about Sofan and view her painting at www.theartofhappiness.net.

Her Facebook and Instagram pages are full of colourful surprises and visual alchemy to make your heart sing. Follow her there now.

Sources And Resources

Gunaratana, Bhante 2011 Mindfulness in plain English, Wisdom

Publications, Somerville, MA USA.

Stahl, Bob & Goldstein, Elisha 2010, A mindfulness-based stress reduction workbook, New Harbinger Publications, California, USA.

Smith, Huston & Novak, Philip 2003, Buddhism: A concise introduction, Harper Collins Publishers, Inc, New York City, USA.

Kornfield, Jack 2009, A path with heart: a guide through the perils and promises of spiritual life, Random House, New York, USA.

Kornfield, Jack 2001, After the ecstasy, the laundry: how the heart grows wise on the spiritual path, Bantam Books, New York City, USA.

Kornfield, Jack 1995, Eightfold path for the householder, Dharma Net

International, Berkeley CA, USA.

Kornfield, Jack 2008, A guide to universal teachings of Buddhist psychology, Bantam Books, New York City, USA.

Stephen Batchelor 1998, Buddhism without beliefs: a contemporary guide to awakening, Riverhead Books, New York City, USA.

Thich Nhat Hanh 2003, *No birth, no death*, Riverhead Books, New York City, USA.

Thich Nhat Hanh 1998, *The heart of the buddha's teaching: transforming suffering into peace, joy, and liberation*, Random House, Hertfordshire, England.

Sumedha, Ajahn Ven. 1992, *The four noble truths*, Amaravati Publications, Hertfordshire, England.

Rahula, Walpola 1978, *What the Buddha taught*, The Gordon Fraser Gallery Ltd, London and Bedford.

Yeshe, Lama 2003, *Becoming your own therapist: make your mind an ocean*, Lama Yeshe Wisdom Archive, Boston, USA.